ULTIMATE JAZZ PLAY-ALONG

Jam with **Eric Marienthal**

B♭ Edition

WARNER BROS. PUBLICATIONS - THE GLOBAL LEADER IN PRINT
USA: 15800 NW 48th Avenue, Miami, FL 33014

WARNER/CHAPPELL MUSIC

CANADA: 85 SCARSDALE ROAD, SUITE 101
DON MILLS, ONTARIO, M3B 2R2
SCANDINAVIA: P.O. BOX 533, VENDEVAGEN 85 B
S-182 15, DANDERYD, SWEDEN
AUSTRALIA: P.O. BOX 353
3 TALAVERA ROAD, NORTH RYDE N.S.W. 2113

Carisch
NUOVA CARISCH

ITALY: VIA M.F. QUINTILIANO 40
20138 MILANO
SPAIN: MAGALLANES, 25
28015 MADRID

IMP
INTERNATIONAL MUSIC PUBLICATIONS LIMITED

ENGLAND: SOUTHEND ROAD,
WOODFORD GREEN, ESSEX IG8 8HN
FRANCE: 25 RUE DE HAUTEVILLE, 75010 PARIS
GERMANY: MARSTALLSTR. 8, D-80539 MÜNCHEN
DENMARK: DANMUSIK, VOGNMAGERGADE 7
DK 1120 KOBENHAVNK

Book Design: Ken Rehm

Published by Manhattan Music Publications Inc.
A Warner Bros. Publications Inc. Company

© 1997 WARNER BROS. PUBLICATIONS
All Rights Reserved

Any duplication, adaptation or arrangement of the compositions
contained in this collection requires the written consent of the Publisher.
No part of this book may be photocopied or reproduced in any way without permission.
Unauthorized uses are an infringement of the U.S. Copyright Act and are punishable by law.

MW00681693

INTRODUCTION

This book is the result of many requests that I've had from students who want to improve their improvising skills. We all know how important it is to have a vehicle that we can use to hone our skills and strengthen our playing. The best possible vehicle would be to have the perfect band to play with whenever you want to work on your soloing. Since that's not always easy to put together, play-along CD's are a very good substitute. The high quality play-along packages that are available today provide a great way to work on your technique and soloing in a practical setting.

The request that most of my students have is that even though they know the chord scales and can read the changes as they go by, they still want some ideas as to what to actually play. It's one thing to know the chord changes of a tune but it's also helpful to have some melodic examples or "licks" that you can use to base your solos around.

This book is my answer to that request and I hope that you will find these solos useful and fun. The idea is to take the recorded play-along concept one step further. This package is a collection of solos written over a series of different chord changes and styles such as straight-ahead jazz, funk, swing, R&B, latin, blues and more. My students have enjoyed and benefited from working with this material and I hope you will too.

HOW TO USE THIS BOOK

The idea of working on these solos is not to memorize them and play them note-for-note in your own improvisations. The best thing to do is to use some of the ideas or "licks" out of these solos to help build your own musical vocabulary. Transcribing solos from records is a very useful way to create your own pool of musical ideas. Use these solos in the same way. Here are some suggestions for getting the most out of this book:

1. Learn each written solo before playing it with the CD so that you aren't struggling to keep up with the tempo of the music. Always try to practice with a metronome to make sure that all the phrases are being played smoothly and accurately.

2. Each track on the CD has a short version to match the length of the written solo and a long version to improvise over. Play the written solo along with the short version of the music so that it sounds like your own solo rather than something that you're reading. Make sure that your time feels good and fits right into the rhythm section.

3. Now play over the long version of the music and instead of reading the solo, improvise your own solo while following the chord changes on the improvising page. When you feel you want to draw from the written solo, look over to the written solo page and use some of those ideas. By playing with the tracks in this way, you can take your favorite licks from the written solos and incorporate them into your own improvisations.

My thanks to Dave Witham for both recording this music and for his great playing on these tracks. Dave's creative input helped me a great deal during the conception of this project. Also, my thanks to Paul Navidad for doing such a good job engraving the music, and to Dan Thress for working so hard in putting this project together.

Good luck!

CONTENTS

AUDIO

CD Play-Along Track

MAJOR CHORD SOLO	(1) short version
CHART	(2) long version
FUNKY MINOR CHORD SOLO	(3) short version
CHART	(4) long version
BLUES SOLO	(5) short version
CHART	(6) long version
II-V-I SOLO	(7) short version
CHART	(8) long version
RHYTHM CHANGES SOLO	(9) short version
CHART	(10) long version
25 LICKS SOLO	(11) short version
CHART	(12) long version
SAMBA MINOR CHORD SOLO	(13) short version
CHART	(14) long version
"DONNA LEE" SOLO	(15) short version
CHART	(16) long version
FUNK IN F MINOR SOLO	(17) short version
CHART	(18) long version
MINOR II-V'S SOLO	(19) short version
CHART	(20) long version
TEXAS SHUFFLE SOLO	(21) short version
CHART	(22) long version
MERCY-ISH	(23) short version
CHART	(24) long version

MAJOR CHORD SOLO

MAJOR CHORD SOLO CHART

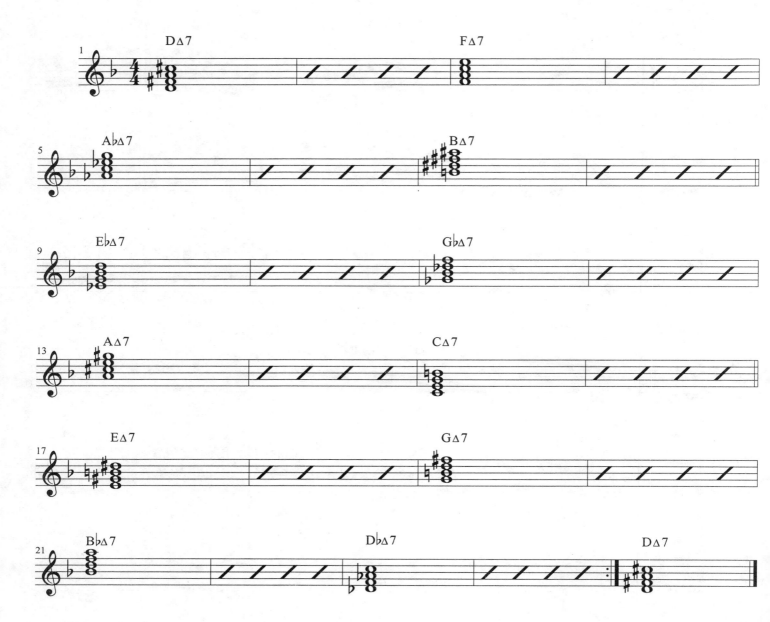

FUNKY MINOR CHORD SOLO

10

FUNKY MINOR CHORD SOLO CHART

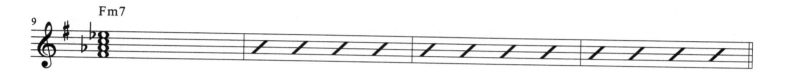

THE BLUES

THE BLUES CHART

II–V–I

II-V-I CHART

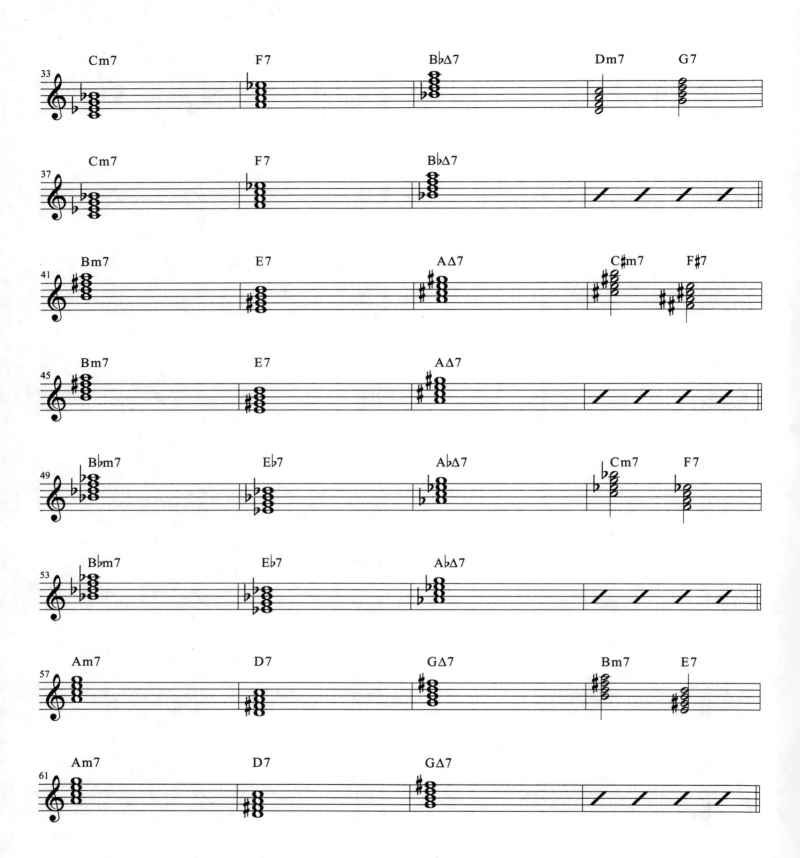

RHYTHM CHANGES SOLO

RHYTHM CHANGES SOLO CHART

25 LICKS

CD
11
Track

24

25 LICKS CHART

SAMBA MINOR CHORD SOLO CHART

26

SAMBA MINOR CHORD SOLO

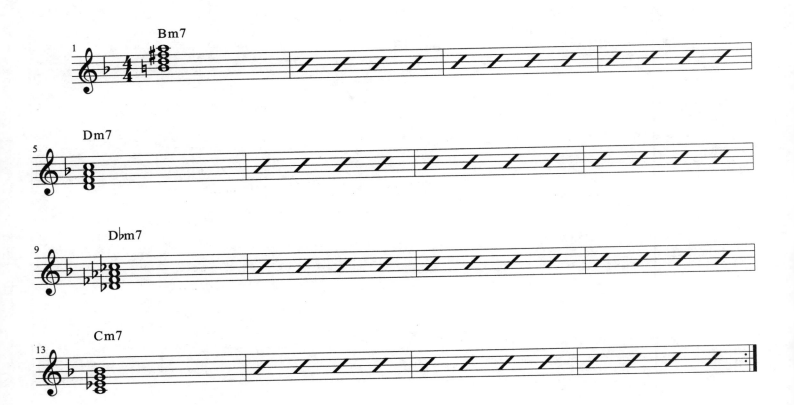

DONNA LEE SOLO

DONNA LEE CHART

FUNK IN G MINOR

FUNK IN G MINOR CHART

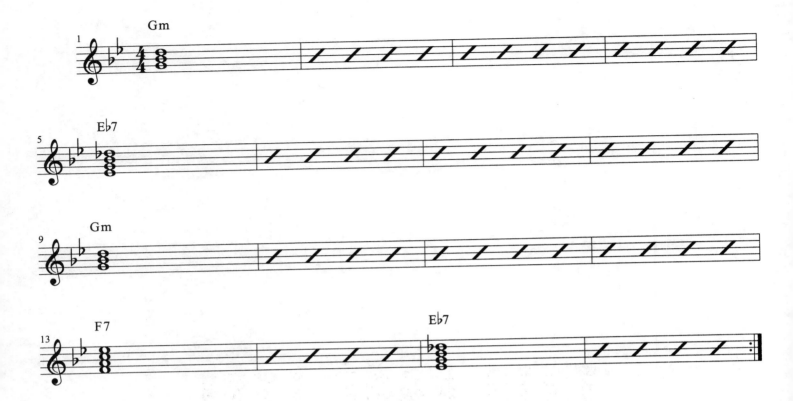

THIS PAGE LEFT
INTENTIONALLY BLANK

MINOR II–V'S

36

MINOR II–V'S CHART

TEXAS SHUFFLE

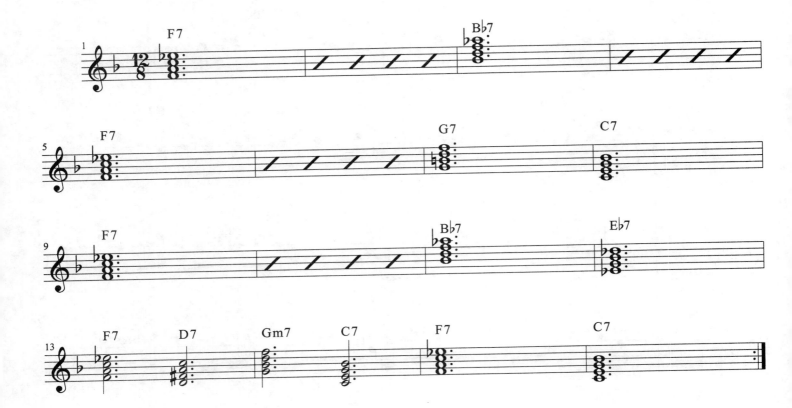

MERCY-ISH

MERCY-ISH CHART

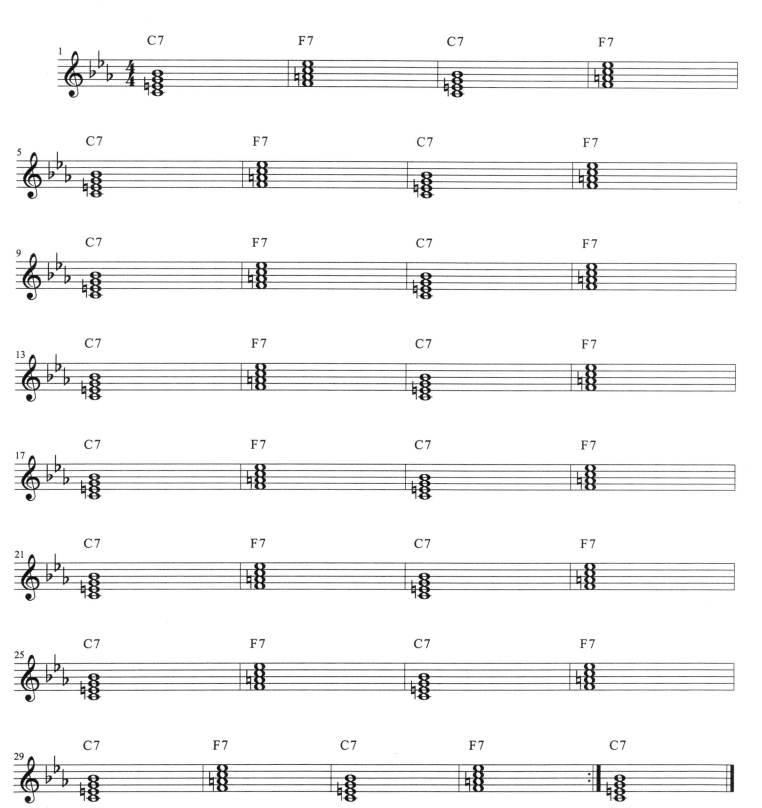

ALSO AVAILABLE FROM ERIC MARIENTHAL AND WARNER BROS. PUBLICATIONS

VIDEOS

Play Sax from Day One is a complete introduction to the saxophone. Starting with an overview of the saxes (soprano, alto, and tenor) then putting the horn together, mouthpieces, reeds, ligature, tone production, fingerings, tonguing and more.
With fingering chart.

Level: Beginner

VH0110 $39.95

Modern Sax features a broad range of tips and techniques for the intermediate to advanced saxophonist. Here Eric offers exercises designed to build technique, methods for extending your range, a discussion of ear training and a detailed overview of improvisation and jazz harmony.

Level: Intermediate

VH0111 $39.95

Tricks of the Trade is a comprehensive study of many of the elements used by today's top jazz improvisers put together in a play-along format. Segments include: playing over changes, creating rhythm in your playing, trick licks, high note licks, growls and multiphonics, and communicating with an audience.
Running time 70 minutes. With booklet.

Level: Intermediate to Advanced

VH0276 $39.95

AVAILABLE AT YOR LOCAL MUSIC RETAILER OR CALL TOLL FREE 1-800-628-1528 EXT. 215/219

ONE-OF-A-KIND SAXOPHONE METHOD AND PERFORMANCE BOOKS FROM WARNER BROS. PUBLICATIONS

Eric Marienthal's Comprehensive Jazz Studies & Exercises

A complete book of jazz technique studies and exercises for all instrumentalists. This text deals with many technique issues jazz musicians encounter in the real world. Topics covered in the book include: Chord Scale Exercises, Motif Exercises, Finger Busters, Extended Motif Exercises, Ideas For Improvisation.

EL96113 $19.95

Sax/Flute Lessons With The Greats

is a one-of-a-kind book/audio package filled with musical examples and a wealth of professional insight and advice. Topics include: reeds, mouthpieces, tone, doubling, playing over chord changes, the altissimo register, recording, rhythm, intonation, modes, as well as the business of music and the future of jazz. The accompanying CD/cassette contains a selection of examples from the book which are played by each of the artists so you can follow along and hear exactly how they should sound.

Book and Cassette MMBK0038AT $21.95
Book and CD MMBK0038CD $24.95

Bob Mintzer
14 Jazz & Funk Etudes,

written by jazz musician Bob Mintzer, 14 Jazz & Funk Etudes presents practice and performance aids and explanations in a variety of jazz and funk styles. In addition, the books include a CD containing combo accompaniment that's ideal for practice sessions. Available in C, B♭, B♭ trumpet, E♭, and bass clef.

$24.95 with CD

AVAILABLE AT YOR LOCAL MUSIC RETAILER
OR CALL TOLL FREE 1-800-628-1528 EXT. 215/219